# The *First* Writing Kit

English Kits is a lively series of structured photocopiable resource books for key areas of primary English. Other English Kits published by Stanley Thornes:

Moira Andrew and David Orme, *The Second Writing Kit*
Moira Andrew and David Orme, *The First Poetry Kit*
  *The Second Poetry Kit*
Helen Hadley, *The First Speaking and Listening Kit*
  *The Second Speaking and Listening Kit*

Moira Andrew • David Orme

Stanley Thornes (Publishers) Ltd

Text © Moira Andrew and David Orme 1992
Original line illustrations © ST(P) Ltd 1992

The right of Moira Andrew and David Orme to be identified as authors of this work has been asserted by them in accordance with the Copyright, Designs and Patents Act 1988.

The copyright holders authorise ONLY users of *The First Writing Kit* to make photocopies or stencil duplicates of the pupils' sheets for their own or their classes' immediate use within the teaching context.

No other rights are granted without permission in writing from the publisher or under licence from the Copyright Licensing Agency Limited. Further details of such licences (for reprographic reproduction) may be obtained from the Copyright Licensing Agency Limited, of 90 Tottenham Court Road, London W1P 9HE.

Copy by any other means or for any other purpose is strictly prohibited without the prior written consent of the copyright holders.

Applications for such permission should be addressed to the publishers: Stanley Thornes (Publishers) Ltd, Old Station Drive, Leckhampton, CHELTENHAM GL53 0DN, England.

First published in 1992 by:
Stanley Thornes (Publishers) Ltd
Old Station Drive
Leckhampton
CHELTENHAM GL53 0DN

A catalogue record for this book is available from the British Library.

ISBN 0 7487 1486 3

The cover photograph is reproduced by courtesy of ZEFA.

Typeset by Tech-Set, Gateshead.
Printed and bound in Great Britain by Ebenezer Baylis, Worcester.

# Contents

| | |
|---|---|
| Introduction | 1 |
| Teacher's Notes | 5 |

**Myself**

| | |
|---|---|
| Portrait of Me | 12 |
| Make a Zigzag Book | 13 |
| Three Wishes | 14 |
| Diary of Yesterday | 15 |
| Fact File | 16 |

**Home and Family**

| | |
|---|---|
| Doll's House | 18 |
| Family Tree | 19 |
| Grandma's Baby | 20 |
| Look Outside | 21 |
| The New Baby | 22 |

**Food**

| | |
|---|---|
| Shopping List | 24 |
| What's Cooking? | 25 |
| Chocolate Crispies | 26 |
| Healthy Eating | 27 |
| Food Prayer | 28 |

**School**

| | |
|---|---|
| Headed Paper | 30 |
| Playground Games | 31 |
| Make a Book | 32 |
| Getting Ready for School | 33 |
| School Rules | 34 |

**Weather**

| | |
|---|---|
| Weather Chart | 36 |
| Weather Invitations | 37 |
| Bear's Clothes | 38 |
| Bear at Granny's House | 39 |
| Weather Words | 40 |

**Seasons**

| | |
|---|---|
| Birthday Calendar | 42 |
| The Apple Tree's Year | 43 |
| Harvest Thanksgiving | 44 |
| Make a Card | 45 |
| A Christmas Diary | 46 |

**Colour**

| | |
|---|---|
| Colour Signals | 48 |
| Rainbows | 49 |
| Invent-a-Colour | 50 |
| At the End of the Rainbow | 51 |
| Make a Garden | 52 |

**Creatures**

| | |
|---|---|
| Name Me, Draw Me | 54 |
| Into the Ark | 55 |
| Space Creatures | 56 |
| Recipe for a Monster | 57 |
| A Very Small Creature's Story | 58 |

# Introduction

*The First Writing Kit* is not intended as a complete infant language course. Rather, it can offer:
- a resource to back up work in all the varieties and styles of writing now required under the National Curriculum at Key Stage 1
- imaginative language work for topic-based approaches
- useful end-on activities for children who have completed a task
- extension work for able children.

A wide range of writing tasks is covered, including descriptive and scientific writing, note-making, simple stories, biography and autobiography. There is a range of practical 'scissor and paper' activities offering a number of unusual and exciting ways to present the finished work. By and large, poetry has been excluded, as this has been thoroughly covered in *The Poetry Kit*. There is plenty of work here to extend knowledge about language and familiarity with simple grammatical ideas for those children who are already beginning to read and write with some degree of fluency.

## Using *The First Writing Kit*

**Preparation**
We have tried to keep instruction on the pupils' sheets to a minimum, and to provide what is required in the Teacher's Notes. Some sheets will require specific preparation by pupils or teacher, and details of this are also included in the Notes. Work on all sheets will benefit from initial discussion with the whole class. Very young children may require further help to ensure that they know exactly what it is they have to do.

**Drafting**
Most sheets are intended to be written on, but a few provide stimulus for writing on a separate sheet. It is good practice in every case to encourage rough drafts on paper before the sheet itself is used.

**Extension**
In most cases the sheets act as the first stage of a more extensive piece of work and suggestions for extension activities are given in the Notes.

## Managing Writing in the Infant Classroom

Children come to school with a willingness to write. They have seen their parents writing and may have tried to scribble 'writing' of their own. To begin with, what they want to say will outstrip their ability to write. We would encourage teachers to act as scribes for young writers in the early stages.

**Scribing**
Working with a group or an individual child, write down their ideas 'as they come' on paper. A 'question and answer' approach will provide a range of ideas. On a second sheet begin to arrange the ideas into some sort of order. Read back what you have written to the children and, when they are satisfied, produce a final copy. Children will be able to 'read' this for themselves.

As their writing skills develop, they will be able to take on increasing responsibility for 'scribing' themselves. From a very early age children should see writing as a process in stages; the simple scribing and arranging process described above is the beginning of the notion of drafting.

## The Stages of Writing

- Inspiration (the initial idea or stimulus)
- Preparation (brainstorming, note-making, discussion, planning)
- Drafting, conferencing
- Presentation
- Assessment

**Inspiration**
The sheets provide a wide range of starter ideas for writing, and will help to develop the pupil's own writing skills. Always try to relate the skills learned to real writing tasks of importance to the child. Work on letters, for example, should lead on to the writing of real letters. Narrative approaches suggested here should be applied to incidents and experiences in the children's own lives.

**Preparation**
Sequential writing will require some sort of planning in advance. Left to their own devices, children will start a story with little thought as to how it might develop. Travelling hopefully in this way can often be fun, but the end result is usually disappointing for the writer and tedious for the teacher. For narrative writing, children will need to think about story structure and the development of characters. For simple accounts of events, or sets of instructions, they will need to discover appropriate forms for the particular task in hand; they will need to know the difference between, for example, a set of cookery instructions, and an account of what took place during the cookery activity. Many forms of writing benefit from a brainstorming session, during which ideas are jotted down as quickly as possible.

**Drafting, Conferencing**
Drafting is a key skill, and its importance is underlined in National Curriculum attainment targets. At Level 3, children are expected to 'Begin to revise and redraft in discussion with the teacher, other adults, or other children in the class, paying attention to meaning and clarity as well as checking for matters such as correct and consistent use of tenses and pronouns.' In our view, simple drafting should start even earlier than this. In theory, this is all well and good, but the practice can cause problems for classroom management.

# Introduction

Poetry is a good activity for working on drafting, as poems are short enough for the child to be willing to rewrite them completely, perhaps a couple of times. Requiring a child to rewrite a relatively lengthy story is a different matter, of course, as the first draft may have been the result of considerable effort. There are also limitations on the time a teacher has to devote to each pupil's conferencing session. All too often 'conferencing' ends up as a session in which technical errors are corrected. Secretarial skills are important, but an ill-thought-out piece of writing is still unsatisfactory, however technically accurate and well-presented it might be.

Possible solutions are:
- emphasising the planning/brainstorming stage. Discussion on, say, writing about characters or story structure in advance will reduce the necessity for fundamental redrafting. The notes produced at this stage can be considered the 'first draft'.
- encouraging a wide range of pieces of work of varying lengths. Shorter pieces can be worked on and redrafted more easily.
- looking for learning points in a piece of writing. In a major piece of writing, it is pointless to try and cover all aspects of language. Pick on just one thing and concentrate on that.
- suggesting that the child works on a redraft of just a section of his or her writing.
- encouraging the use of the word processor; this makes the drafting process far simpler.
- providing attractive and unusual ways of presenting the final draft; a book or wall display are possibilities. This gives the final draft a real purpose.
- conferencing at various stages in the writing. A 'where do we go from here?' conference is more productive than a 'where did we go wrong?' one.
- group and pair writing. Writing in co-operation with other children allows for a process of continuous conferencing. In the Teacher's Notes we have indicated where group and pair writing work particularly well.

**Presentation**
'Presentation' is sometimes used to mean the production of a neat copy, perhaps tastefully illustrated. We would encourage teachers to take a broader view of presentation, taking in the notion of writing for an audience. In a writer's mind should be the questions, 'Who am I writing for?' and 'What is the best way of presenting my writing for them?' The answer may well be a neat, illustrated copy, but other possibilities are:
- individual 'bookmaking'. A folded piece of paper makes a simple four-page 'book'. The 'front cover' can be for the title and author's name; the story or poem can then spread on to the other three pages, with suitable illustrations. The addition of a second sheet will produce a more sophisticated product, and will introduce the idea of binding. The completed books can be displayed. A number of the sheets in this book lend themselves to the 'book' approach.
- a reading or performance, either live or on tape or video, by the pupils or teacher. In the early stages children may lack the confidence and skill to read in public, but will enjoy a reading by the teacher. As confidence develops, this is another area where children can gradually assume responsibility.
- a publication, such as a class booklet or anthology.
- a wall display covering a particular topic.

## The Role of the Teacher

The teacher's role has changed over the years from a didactic to an enabling one. Enabling should not be seen as being uninvolved in the writing process. Teachers need to be involved by:
- initiating the writing process, perhaps by providing the stimulus or by drawing children's attention to the writing possibilities in their own lives
- being involved in the preparations for writing, perhaps by leading a class or group brainstorming session
- providing writing structures such as those in *The First Writing Kit* within which children can work and gain confidence
- providing an appropriate environment for writing
- providing models and examples
- taking on the role of scribe
- providing a context in which children can present their work.

## Knowledge about Language

Knowledge about language covers forms of language – note-making, letters, diaries, interpretation of charts and diagrams, speech, formal or informal talk – and more detailed knowledge about the nuts and bolts of language: punctuation, sentence building, story structure, use of tense, development of an appropriate vocabulary, and so on. The grid on page 4 shows which aspects of knowledge about language are emphasised on each page of *The First Writing Kit*.

## Secretarial Skills

These include spelling, layout, presentation, and the ability to use 'standard English'. It is important that the right balance is struck between the various skills of writing. Frequently literacy is equated in the mind of the public and in the media with a high level of secretarial skill. This is frequently what people mean when they complain of 'poor grammar'. In fact, poor secretarial skills rarely prevent a piece of writing from fulfilling its function. Poor spelling or an inability to use, say, inverted commas correctly may be irritating, but the greengrocer's use of 'carrot's' does not prevent us finding out what is on offer.

Nevertheless, secretarial skills are important, and it is a calumny on teachers to suggest that they think these things 'do not matter'. What is important is *when* they matter, which is at

# Introduction

the presentational stage of the writing process. Infants should be encouraged to get ideas down first; so many good ideas vanish while the child is looking for a spelling. Encourage the use of the 'magic line' (suggested in the National Writing Project) in which the child writes as much of the word as he or she can and inserts a line for the rest. The spelling can then be sorted out later.

Once children are conscious of an audience they will see the value of producing a final draft that is neat, well laid out, and correct, although the degree of 'correctness' will increase as the child progresses. They will enjoy seeing their work written out for them by the teacher or word-processed, and this is to be encouraged.

## Assessment

Whether or not creative writing can be assessed is a subject for much disagreement. The general view is that the more 'imaginative' a piece of writing is, the more the response becomes a subjective one. For an exercise in letter writing or a set of instructions, it is relatively easy to provide a checklist of criteria against which the writing can be judged. In creative writing such as stories or poems there are assessable elements, but it is difficult to provide a yardstick for an outcome when frequently the best writing is the most unexpected. The best yardstick that can be applied is the child's work as a whole – does this piece of work demonstrate development, a steady growth of confidence and skill? A subjective assessment should not be dismissed. As a teacher, it is worth asking:
- How do I feel about this piece of writing? Am I excited, bored, interested, pleased?
- How did the writer feel about it?
- If there is an audience (and there should be), how did they react to the piece of writing?

## *The First Writing Kit* and the National Curriculum

*The First Writing Kit* has been designed to enable children to work towards the attainment targets demanded by the National Curriculum at Key Stage 1, Levels 1 to 3.

### Speaking and Listening
The activities in *The First Writing Kit* should enable children to:
- participate as speakers and listeners in group activities (L1)
- describe an event, real or imagined, to a teacher or other pupil (L2).

### Writing
The activities in *The First Writing Kit* should enable children to:
- use pictures, symbols or isolated letters, words or phrases to communicate meaning (L1)
- produce independently, pieces of writing using complete sentences, some of them demarcated with capital letters and full stops or question marks (L1)
- structure sequences of real or imagined events coherently in chronological accounts (L2)
- write stories showing an understanding of the rudiments of story structure by establishing an opening, characters, and one or more events (L2)
- produce simple, coherent non-chronological writing (L2).

# Introduction

## Key Elements in the Pupils' Sheets

| | Letter Writing | Instructional Writing | Biography | Autobiography | Research/Handling Information | Narrative | Imaginative | Note Making | Diary Writing | Vocabulary Building | Display Activity |
|---|---|---|---|---|---|---|---|---|---|---|---|
| **Myself** | | | | | | | | | | | |
| Portrait of Me | | | | ✓ | | | | ✓ | | | |
| Make a Zigzag Book | | | | | | | | | | ✓ | ✓ |
| Three Wishes | | | | | | | ✓ | | | | |
| Diary of Yesterday | | | | | ✓ | | | | ✓ | | |
| Fact File | | | | ✓ | ✓ | | | ✓ | | | |
| **Home and Family** | | | | | | | | | | | |
| Doll's House | | | | | | | | | | ✓ | ✓ |
| Family Tree | | | ✓ | | ✓ | | | | | | |
| Grandma's Baby | | | ✓ | | ✓ | | | | | | |
| Look Outside | | | | | | ✓ | ✓ | | | | |
| The New Baby | ✓ | | | | ✓ | | | | | ✓ | ✓ |
| **Food** | | | | | | | | | | | |
| Shopping List | | | | | ✓ | | | | | ✓ | |
| What's Cooking? | | ✓ | | | | | | | | ✓ | ✓ |
| Chocolate Crispies | | ✓ | | | ✓ | | | ✓ | | | |
| Healthy Eating | | | | | ✓ | | | | | ✓ | ✓ |
| Food Prayer | | | | | | | ✓ | | | | ✓ |
| **School** | | | | | | | | | | | |
| Headed Paper | ✓ | | | | | | | | | | ✓ |
| Playground Games | | ✓ | | | ✓ | | | | | | ✓ |
| Make a Book | | | | | | | | | | ✓ | ✓ |
| Getting Ready for School | | | | | | ✓ | | | | | ✓ |
| School Rules | | ✓ | | | | | | | | | |
| **Weather** | | | | | | | | | | | |
| Weather Chart | | ✓ | | | ✓ | | | | | | ✓ |
| Weather Invitations | ✓ | | | | | | ✓ | | | | |
| Bear's Clothes | | | | | | | | | | ✓ | ✓ |
| Bear at Granny's House | | ✓ | | | | | | | | ✓ | ✓ |
| Weather Words | | | | | | | ✓ | | | ✓ | |
| **Seasons** | | | | | | | | | | | |
| Birthday Calendar | | | | | ✓ | | | | | | ✓ |
| The Apple Tree's Year | | | | | ✓ | ✓ | | | | ✓ | ✓ |
| Harvest Thanksgiving | | | | | | | | | | ✓ | ✓ |
| Make a Card | | | | | ✓ | | | | | | ✓ |
| A Christmas Diary | | | | | | | | | ✓ | | ✓ |
| **Colour** | | | | | | | | | | | |
| Colour Signals | | | | | ✓ | | | | | | |
| Rainbows | | | | | ✓ | | | | | ✓ | ✓ |
| Invent-a-Colour | | ✓ | | | | | | ✓ | | | |
| At the End of the Rainbow | | | | | | ✓ | ✓ | | | | ✓ |
| Make a Garden | | | | | ✓ | | | ✓ | | | |
| **Creatures** | | | | | | | | | | | |
| Name Me, Draw Me | | | | | ✓ | | | | | ✓ | |
| Into the Ark | | | | | ✓ | | | | ✓ | ✓ | |
| Space Creatures | | | ✓ | | | ✓ | ✓ | | | | |
| Recipe for a Monster | | ✓ | | | | | ✓ | | | | |
| A Very Small Creature's Story | | | | | ✓ | ✓ | ✓ | | | | ✓ |

# Teacher's Notes and Extension Ideas

## Myself

**Portrait of Me**

This exercise is designed to encourage the children to work on an autobiographical theme. Use mirrors to establish hair colour, eye colour, etc. Discussion should lead them to talk about differences – no two pairs of blue eyes are exactly the same shade. Make a word list from the oral work so that children can fill in the sheet independently.

Under the heading 'Other things about me' it is intended that the children should list things about themselves to enable an artist to draw a picture without seeing them.

Follow up by getting the children to paint portraits of one another from the pen portraits. Make elaborate frames and hang in a 'gallery' in the corridor.

**Make a Zigzag Book**

Use the PE slot to find out as many ways of moving as possible. Make a list of movement words and illustrate with pin men so that the children can use them in independent writing. Make zigzag books by folding A4 paper as shown.

Follow up by getting the children to write zigzag books about animals and insects, e.g. Worms can wriggle, Squirrels can leap, Swallows can swoop, Butterflies can glide, etc. This exercise is designed to extend children's everyday language of movement beyond the simple use of 'go' or 'went'.

Make a large zigzag book to stand behind a display on the nature table.

**Three Wishes**

Tell the story of Aladdin. Talk about what the children would wish for if they could have anything they liked. It might be useful to extend their wishes towards the thought of helping children who are less fortunate than themselves. Get them to complete the sheet with their three wishes.

Follow up with an RE project using packs from Oxfam, Save the Children, etc.

Make a magic carpet wall display with collage cut-outs of all the children's wishes conjured up by Aladdin's genie.

**Diary of Yesterday**

This task is similar to writing up a news book, but through discussion, the children are asked to focus on particular events and feelings. Use a tape recorder. Get children to work in groups of four, one talking about ordinary day-to-day things, one talking about weather and clothes, one talking about unusual events (birthdays, new baby, etc.), and one talking about feelings.

The children should use these ideas to write the diary of yesterday. Those who are not yet able to write for themselves might draw pictures of yesterday's events, the teacher underwriting to the children's dictation.

Frame the diaries using bright felt-tips and package the writing with photographs, headlines from yesterday's newspaper, a TV programme magazine, sweet and biscuit wrappers, drawings of what the children are wearing, etc. Make a 'Class Memories' treasure chest and bury it in the school grounds. Mark the place.

**Fact File**

It is important that young children are able to quote their own address and other details. This task gives them an opportunity to fill in a personal form, a style of writing which, like it or not, is a part of modern life.

A follow-up to this activity might be to produce a birthday pie chart or a street/address graph for the class, using information collected from the fact file forms.

## Home and Family

**Doll's House**

This kind of activity helps with phonic work, especially with 'key' sounds. Get the children to talk about kinds of furniture usually associated with different rooms in the house. Work out how many things they can find beginning with a particular sound. See which sound ends up with the longest list. Use these furniture words to complete the sheet. The children should first colour the pictures on the sheet, label them, cut them out and stick them in the appropriate rooms. They can then go on to draw pictures of other things on their lists, label them and stick them in the rooms.

Make a castle, fairground or seaside outline with cut-out pictures and matching labels. Wall pictures of this kind can make a mini-thesaurus to go with current class themes and projects.

**Family Tree**

Work out a simple questionnaire with the children before beginning this project, so that they can find out the names of people in their families. Using information collected from his or her own family, each child can complete the tree on the sheet to get some sense of a personal history. They can then decorate the tree with leaves and flowers.

Follow up by collecting photographs, drawing pictures, writing poems, etc. about members of the family. Put the photographs, etc. on a time-line. See who can go back furthest in time.

Make an anthology of poems about grandmothers, grandfathers, uncles and aunts. Look in published books and/or make up your own. Draw pictures to go with the poems.

**Grandma's Baby**

Encourage the children to ask their own grandmothers, if possible, about their babies, using the questions on the sheet as a guide. It might be possible to have a grandmother come in to school to talk about her own children. Have the grown-up 'baby' in as well. Make this a question and answer session. Discuss the similarities and differences in how babies were looked

# Teacher's Notes and Extension Ideas

after then and now. Get the children to make notes on a separate sheet before writing their stories.

Get the children to make their stories about Grandma's Baby into books with illustrations.

Follow up the written work with a display showing babywear, photographs, books, toys, etc. from the time contemporary mothers were babies. Emphasise the continuation of the family where appropriate; otherwise show how families move away and begin new lives away from their own childhood homes. Good discussion point: Would you move away? Stay nearby? Why?

**Look Outside**
Working in groups, the children should look out of the classroom window and make notes about all the things they can see. Talk about the sounds these things make or how they move. Make the phrases into a list, e.g. a dog barking, a door opening, a car speeding, etc.

Draw the children's attention to the rhythm of the phrases as they say them aloud and decide how to fill in the spaces on the sheet from their lists. Get them to write out their lists in their best handwriting on another sheet of paper, place the paper beneath the window picture, and staple it in position so that the window can be cut open to reveal the list poems.

Make another list poem, but this time using a door opening on to a magic garden. What might you see? What sounds would you hear? Insert the poem into a door picture.

Make a set of opening poems and display as a class frieze.

**The New Baby**
If any child in the class has had a new baby in the family, get him or her to talk about it. Talk about ways in which he or she can help mum and dad. Talk about the baby's name. Think of the things a new baby needs. Encourage them to make notes. Get all the children to imagine they have a new baby in their house, so they can write the letter to Aunt Anne.

Before tackling the letter, show how a letter is headed with address and post code. Get the children to find their own addresses from their fact file forms. Copy out neatly. Then rough out a letter about the new baby, real or imagined. Copy out in best handwriting on to the sheet.

Try other letters – to Father Christmas, to the school cook, to children in a parallel class in another school, to someone who has helped in the classroom, etc. Get children used to setting out a letter and addressing an envelope properly.

Post some of the letters for real so that they are answered.

## Food

**Shopping List**
Talk about going shopping, likes and dislikes. Why should we make a list before we go to the supermarket? Get the children to work out a shopping list for Mrs Winter – then their own, money no object! They can draw the things on their list in the trolley.

Get them to make another list, e.g. Christmas presents, what they need to pack for their summer holiday, clothes for a school trip, etc.

Make a list of ten things each child would want to take from home, if he or she were invited on a trip to space or to a desert island. Illustrate the lists, collage style, inside the outline of a case, a duffle bag, a net bag, etc. Make a wall frieze.

**What's Cooking?**
Encourage the children to imagine they are running their own cafe or Burger Bar. What favourite foods would they have on the menu? Make a list of food words so that children can fill in the menu on the sheet independently. They can then draw the food on a separate sheet of paper, positioning it so that it can be stapled behind the main sheet. The oven door can then be cut and folded as indicated to reveal the food.

Make up a menu for the Teddy Bears' Picnic. Remember that the food must be easy to carry and can be eaten outside.

Make up a play about the Teddy Bears' Picnic.

**Chocolate Crispies**
Children might be able to work with parent helpers to follow the Chocolate Crispie recipe. Look through recipe books to find some other non-cook recipes which children might be able to make on their own, in order to complete the sheet.

Produce cakes, sweets, etc. for Christmas boxes for OAPs and children in hospital. Organise a cafe for Parents' Evening.

Make up a really horrible recipe for a Monster Party, a Dracula Dance, a Wizards' Convention!

**Healthy Eating**
As preparation, invite the school nurse to talk with the children about healthy and unhealthy foods, and not eating too much of anything! With her help, fill in the poster.

As a follow-up, decide on some of the things that could go in a 'healthy' lunch box. Make up a menu for each day of the school week.

**Food Prayer**
Talk about foods we like to eat, those that are good and bad for us, etc. Talk about children who don't have enough to eat. Look at some of the Oxfam and Save the Children materials. Think about how lucky we are. Get the children to make up prayers of thanks for the food we eat and write them on the sheets. Copy them out on A3 paper and decorate. Read the prayers at assembly. Use the food prayers as part of the Harvest Thanksgiving celebration.

# Teacher's Notes and Extension Ideas

## School

**Headed Paper**
Look at your school notepaper. Discuss with the children why the heading was chosen. Have a competition to design a new heading which has something to do with the name or location of the school. Get the children to write letters on their new headed paper – to parents and friends.

Let the children design personal notepaper to reflect their own name or show a picture of something they enjoy doing, e.g. spade, fork and seed packet for Michael Gardiner; ballet shoes for someone who likes dancing; smiling toes for Horace Proudfoot, etc. Design headed paper for The Queen or the Prime Minister to use.

**Playground Games**
Ask children to bring a selection of things to play with. Look for variety: balls, hoops, marbles, ropes, conkers, scraps, etc. Discuss the games they play outside. Do they know of any others? Get them to ask their parents and grandparents to tell them about games they used to play. How do today's games differ? Build up word lists and ask children to fill in the sheets. Work in pairs.

In the games hall the children might like to invent a new game without props. Make it one which has a clear set of rules. Write down the rules so that another class in the school can follow them.

**Make a Book**
Another exercise to help with key phonics. Discuss the things the children like to do in school so that they can complete the sheet. Move on from the 'I like . . .' phrase to 'We don't like . . ., but . . .' so that the sentences are extended.

Make a book, cutting and folding the pages as shown. For the children who are ready to write on their own, a small book provides opportunities to work at their own rate, using known phrases and experimenting with language. Suggest a range of titles: 'When I was only two', 'I wish I was', 'When I grow up'. On every page use repetitive phrases which can be extended by the children. Books which are quickly finished give the children confidence in writing – even if it was not completely successful, they can have another go in the next one!

**Getting Ready for School**
This exercise emphasises the importance of sequencing in storytelling. Get the children to work out the picture sequence, putting the correct numbers in the boxes, and then think about what happened next. They should then put their own pictures in boxes 5 and 6. Colour, cut out and paste on another piece of paper like a comic strip. Get them to tell the story of the morning underneath the pictures.

Cut up comic strip stories, deleting the last two pictures. Get children, working in pairs, to sequence and finish the stories in their own way, then tell the new story to the others. Make up a book of comic strip stories. (This is an excellent way of finding out if children have followed a story told in assembly – and it is a task which they find enjoyable!)

Make wall displays of Cinderella, the Three Little Pigs, etc. in comic strip style, each group contributing part of the story.

**School Rules**
Talk about the school rules and why we must have them. Emphasise the safety aspect. Talk about the rules in your school. Talk about rules that the family might make at home. If each child could choose just one new rule, what would it be? And why? Talk about the special problems posed by Animal School. Work out new rules for other animals.

Make a collage picture of animals each with a speech bubble shouting out its own special rule.

## Weather

**Weather Chart**
Children are familiar with the symbols used on television weather maps. Gather ideas for rain, sun and snow symbols which they would like to use on their own charts. Get children to work in groups for this exercise. At the end of the week use the chart to extract information for the weather table.

Use the weather chart as a starter for a music or PE lesson. Think of the movement of snow in a blizzard and when it first begins to fall; think of rain as a gentle shower and when it is coming down 'cats and dogs'; think of the movement of trees in a spring breeze and in a gale, etc. Get children to move/dance using all the floor space. Look for words to express each movement. Make up a song using weather sounds or use percussion instruments: the crash of thunder, the flash of lightning, the murmur of raindrops, the drumming of rain in a storm, etc.

**Weather Invitations**
Bring in party and wedding invitations. Look at the information needed: date, time, place, what the event is (party, picnic, barbecue, visit to seaside, etc.). Use this as a basis for children to write to the snow inviting it to fall on their home on Christmas Day. They can follow up by writing to the sun asking it to shine on their birthday, on their summer holiday, for the School Fair, etc.

Write letters inviting parents to a school event. Make them in a suitable shape: a Christmas star, an Easter egg, etc. Ask the parents to write a reply.

**Bear's Clothes**
Talk about the different kinds of clothes we wear to suit the weather. Talk about the need for protection from the cold, the heat and the wet. Discuss the kinds of clothes children like best: colours, materials and fashion. Get the children to colour in the coat for a cold day. Then design Bear's clothes for sun, cold and rain. Cut them out. (Don't forget the shoulder tabs.) Colour the bear shape and paste on to card. Cut out. Make a wardrobe of clothes for all occasions.

# Teacher's Notes and Extension Ideas

Make a display of shoes (sandals, wellies, etc.) and hats (sun hats, hoods, sou'westers, etc.) for various kinds of weather. Find information books and stories to go with the display and make a tape of weather poems.

**Bear at Granny's House**
Many children will have stayed with their grandparents and will know about taking clothes to suit all weathers. Talk about the things they must take with them and why. This task gives practice in writing instructions. Encourage children to make notes in an economical way, so that they give essential information only.

Get the children to make a seaside picture and write a story about Bear's terrible day. Get them to imagine all the disasters that could happen – falling into the sea fully dressed, ice-cream upside down in the sand, getting lost, etc. Imagine what Granny has to say! Make the story into a comic strip.

Using speech balloons from the Seaside Disaster Day story, write a dialogue scene with Granny and Bear. Introduce other characters, e.g. deck chair man, Punch and Judy puppeteer, etc.

**Weather Words**
This exercise will build up into a mini-thesaurus of weather words. Encourage a brainstorming session to think of words to describe the way weather moves, the sounds and colours, how you feel, etc. Make lists under different weather headings. Let children fill in the sheet with words and pictures of their own choosing.

Follow up with weather stories. Encourage children to use some of the descriptive words suggested in the oral session.

## Seasons

**Birthday Calendar**
Collect all the birthday dates of children in the class. Mark the names in on the calendar. Use it to find out which month has most birthdays, which least. Think about the babies born on hot summer days and on cold winter days. Get the children to ask their mums if they remember what the weather was like on the day their baby was born.

Make a pie chart of birthdays from the calendar. Think of other ways of presenting this information, e.g. a bar chart. Make wall charts of class birthdays using as many different ways of showing information as possible.

**The Apple Tree's Year**
Get the children to think of how the apple tree changes during the year. Let them use coloured pencils to show how the tree looks at each different season from blossom in spring to bare branches in winter-time. Make the pictures into a zigzag book.

Discuss words which describe the tree through the seasons, e.g. ripe, bare, blossom, buds, fruit, bees, pollen, etc. Make a word list and get the children to write a story of the apple tree's year in the space provided on the sheet.

Follow up by collecting words to go with the sequence of egg, caterpillar, butterfly; spawn, tadpole, frog; chestnut tree through the year, etc. Make zigzag books.

**Harvest Thanksgiving**
On the morning of the harvest service, look at all the gifts on the harvest table. Encourage the children to think about where everything originated – garden, hedgerows, the sea, shops. Make lists of harvest words. Use the lists to write about harvest-time.

Get the children to make a selection of other four-paged books in the shape of something brought in to celebrate harvest: a loaf of bread, a tomato, a blackberry, a fish. Write a sentence on each page and draw pictures to go with the writing.

Make a wall collage of harvest gifts, each fruit, vegetable, flower individually painted and cut out. Paste into a large basket outline and pin the children's books beneath the frieze.

**Make a Card**
Bring a collection of cards to school. Talk about the special days they celebrate. Why do we send cards? When is a card preferable to a letter? Make a list of events for which cards might be made: birthday, wedding, Christmas, Easter, Diwali, Jewish New Year, Mother's Day, etc. Talk about the greetings we send and make a list with the children. Make a card from the pattern on the sheet. Choose a greeting. Decorate.

Make a range of greeting cards and set up a shop in the classroom. Price the cards and take turns to buy and sell.

**A Christmas Diary**
Get the children to use the sheet to make a diary for Father or Mother Christmas in the busy week up to and including Christmas. Think about all the things they will have to do. Think about the weather, about mapping the route, feeding the reindeer. The diary could be made into an advent calendar, with opening doors.

Make a similar diary for Noah, Winne the Pooh, characters in *The Wind in the Willows* or Mr Spock. Keep it short, a week at most. Cut the diary into a suitable shape, e.g. a boat for the river animals, a spaceship for Mr Spock.

Children might like to keep their own mini-diary of the days before Christmas, during the school holidays, when they move house, etc.

## Colour

**Colour Signals**
Talk about traffic lights, what they tell us and why they must be obeyed. Talk about other ways in which coloured lights

# Teacher's Notes and Extension Ideas

give signals, e.g. blue flashing lights on fire tenders, police cars, ambulances. What message do Christmas tree lights and coloured street decorations give us? Think of other lights which help us.

Make a street scene frieze with shop lights, street lights, traffic lights, etc. Use a black background and make the street look very colourful.

Find out how coloured flags are used for signalling. Make a set of coloured flags using a different design for each letter of the alphabet. Use the flags to spell out a class message, e.g. Happy Christmas, Welcome Back Miss Allen, Enjoy Your Easter Holidays, etc. Be sure to put a key near the display.

### Rainbows

Look at pictures of rainbows – better still, interrupt the class if you see one through the window. Talk about the colours. Discuss what colour indigo is. Let the children colour the rainbow using crayons.

Talk about things that are always red, yellow, green, blue. Ask the children if they can think of anything other than an orange that is orange in colour. Get them to draw and name the things they have found on the sheet.

Use their ideas to make a poem about one colour. For example, a poem entitled 'What is red?' could use the ideas in a list like this:

> 'Red is a geranium,
> growing in the sun.
> Red is a danger light
> warning cars to stop.'

Make displays of red, blue, green and yellow to go with the poems.

Talk about the shape of a rainbow. Get the children to think of anything else it looks like: a bridge, a slide, a tunnel? Write a poem beginning 'A rainbow is like a candy-striped bridge . . .' Encourage them to find different ways to finish the poem, working in groups.

### Invent-a-Colour

Get the children to think of a colour that is absolutely new, and to make it using three different colours, one on top of the other. Pencil crayons or oil-based pastels are best. Get them to think of a name for their new colour. Let them work in pairs and try to write down the recipe for their new colour. Can the partner follow the instructions?

Get the children to invent a new animal, and to think about a new shape and colour for their animal. Make lots of different animals and design a Wildlife Park where the new animals can roam free.

### At the End of the Rainbow

Find a story about the pot of gold at the end of the rainbow – or make up one of your own! Look at Sam and Claire's story and get the children to work in groups to finish the comic strips. Get the class back together to talk about all the different endings they came up with.

The children could now tell Sam and Claire's story in a different way – as a poem, a song, a play or a story. Use lots of dialogue by looking at the words in the speech bubbles.

### Make a Garden

Look at several flower shapes, preferably using real flowers. Find words to describe the shapes. Look at mathematical shapes using objects around the classroom. Make a list of shape and colour words so that the children can use the sheets independently. Get them to work in pairs for this exercise so that they have practice in writing and in following instructions.

Follow up by making a garden frieze using round poppy shapes, spiky daisy shapes and bell flowers. Use a collage technique.

## Creatures

### Name Me, Draw Me

Talk about the special characteristics by which we recognise individual animals. Look at pictures in reference books. Talk about camouflage, how it works, why it is necessary. Get the children to draw and write about the animals on the sheet.

Let them invent their own animal for the last space. Make it quite fantastic: spotted in purple and green, neck like a dinosaur, wings like a dragon perhaps!

In groups, the children could make up a brochure for a Fantasy Wildlife Park. Explain all the things visitors can do and see. Draw pictures of the animals who live there.

### Into the Ark

Make up a set of movement words and match them to the animals who went into the ark. Encourage the children to search for as many different ways of expressing movement as they can, e.g. snake – wriggle, slide, slither, glide, etc.

Get the children to use these words to make up a story or diary for the animals at sea in the ark for forty days and forty nights. Encourage them to think how frightened the animals must have been, how crowded together under the decks, how arguments must have broken out between them, how much they must have longed to be on dry land again.

### Space Creatures

Look at reference books to see the ways in which different habitats and life styles are described for various animals.

Talk with the children about the best way of describing a creature that nobody except you has ever seen. Would you take a photograph? Draw a picture? Tape record the sound it makes?

Working in groups let them make a model of a space creature that they have discovered. Put it in a rocky, silver, bone-white or green environment. Following the headings on the sheet, they can then write a descriptive label to put beside the space creature.

# Teacher's Notes and Extension Ideas

**Recipe for a Monster**

Look at recipe books to see the way a recipe is set out. Encourage the children to think of all the biggest things in the world that could go towards making their monster, e.g. a head as big as a boulder, a mountain top or a double decker bus. How long would it take to cook a monster? 24 hours? a week? a year? a century? How would you decorate it? stars for eyes? icicles for teeth? wings sprinkled with gold dust? Think fantastic! Get the children to think of a name for their monster.

Follow up by getting the children to make a very long zigzag book with all the parts of the monster described on each page. Use paints or felt tips to illustrate it, joining the picture edge to edge.

**A Very Small Creature's Story**

Talk about the very smallest creatures the children can think of: ladybird, ant, woodlouse, cricket, etc. Get them to use reference books to discover as much as they can about them. They can then cut and fold the page to make a tiny book for their tiny creature. Make a library of little books and keep them in a decorated box. Let the children read their little creature stories to the youngest children in the school.

# Myself

# Portrait of Me

My name is _____

I am _____ years old.

My eyes are _____

My hair is _____

I like to wear _____

My favourite colour is _____

My best thing at school is

_____

I like to eat _____

_____

I don't like to eat _____

_____

Other things about me

_____

_____

_____

_____

_____

**Portrait of** _____

# Make a Zigzag Book

Choose some of the words below to write in your zigzag book. Draw a picture to match your writing.

run　hop　march　dance　skip　swim　roll　jump　crawl　climb

13

---

My I can
Zigzag
Book

I can _____

I can _____

I can _____

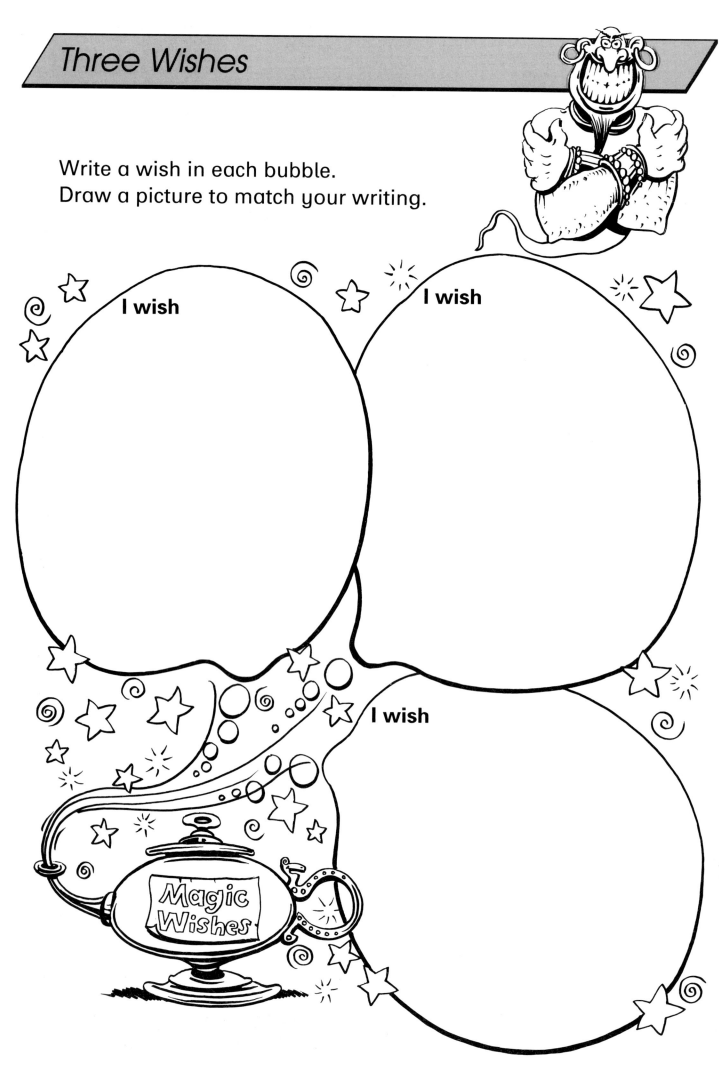

## Diary of Yesterday

What did you do yesterday? Think about:

ordinary things, unusual things,
sad things, happy things,
the weather, your clothes.

Write a diary of yesterday.

*Yesterday*   **Date:**

# Fact File

My name: _____

My address: _____
_____
_____

Postcode: _____

My birthday: _____

Names of people in my family: _____
_____
_____
_____

My school address: _____
_____
_____

Postcode: _____

My teacher's name: _____

My headteacher's name: _____

Today is: _____

Some of the things we do in school today: _____
_____
_____
_____

# Home and Family

# Doll's House

Colour and cut out the pictures.
Paste each picture into its own room.
Label the pictures.

ch _ _ _

t _ _ _ _

l _ _ _

b _ _

b _ _ _

Put more things in the house. Name them.

18

# Family Tree

Find out the names of people in your family. Write the names in the right spaces on the tree.

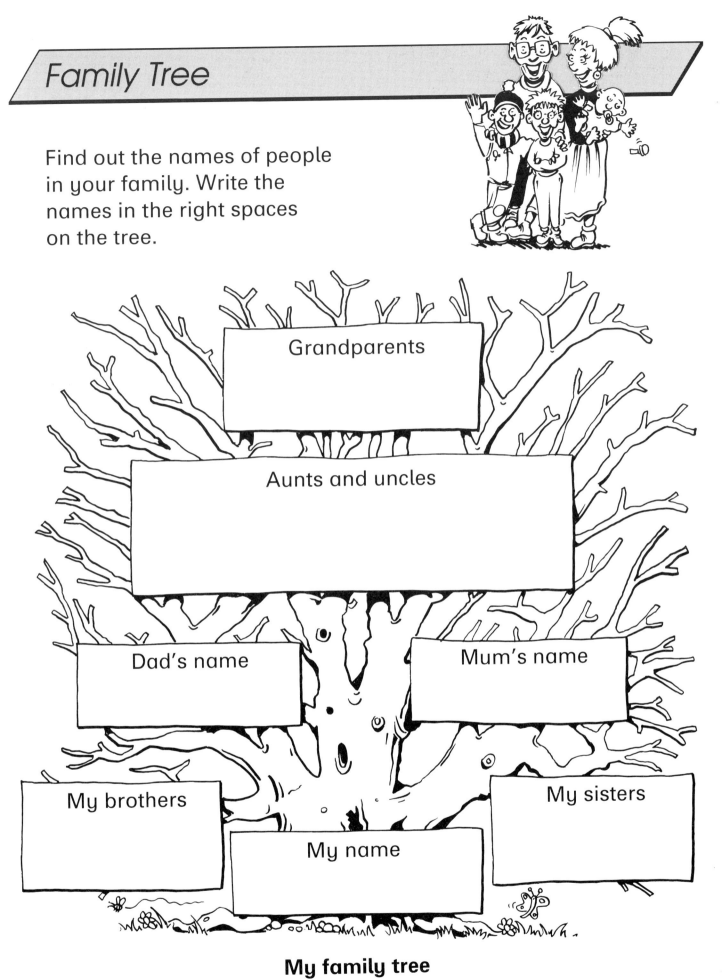

**My family tree**

Put in all the family names you can find.
Draw leaves and flowers on the tree.

# Grandma's Baby

Ask Grandma to tell you about her baby – your mum or dad! Make notes. Ask her these questions:

What did the baby look like?
What clothes did the baby wear?
What were the baby's first words?
What naughty things did the baby do?

Look for photographs of Grandma's baby and make your notes into a story with pictures.

**Grandma's Baby**

# Look Outside

Look out of the window to make a poem. Make a list of some of the things you can see. Then write what they do, like this:

a bird flying

a flower _ _ _ _ ing

a child _ _ _ _ ing

# The New Baby

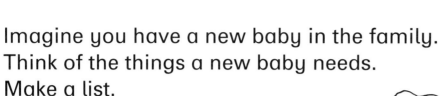

Imagine you have a new baby in the family.
Think of the things a new baby needs.
Make a list.

Choose a name for your new baby.

Aunt Anne lives in Australia. Write a letter telling her all about the baby. Draw a picture to show her what the baby looks like.

Dear Aunt Anne,

# Food

# Shopping List

Here is Mrs Winter's shopping!
Can you write her shopping list?

**Mrs Winter's shopping list**

Now write a list of the things you would like to buy from the supermarket, and draw them in the empty trolley.

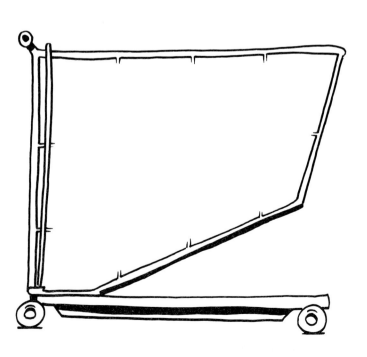

**My shopping list**

# What's Cooking?

What are you having for dinner? Write the menu on the door of the oven. You can draw your dinner inside the oven.

# Chocolate Crispies

Here is a recipe for chocolate crispies. It is in two parts. This recipe will make enough for ten people. (You might need a grown-up to help.)

**Things you need:**

7 tablespoons of Rice Crispies or Cornflakes
1 level tablespoon of cocoa
1 tablespoon of icing sugar
1 tablespoon golden syrup
25 grammes of margarine

**How to cook:**

1. Melt the margarine, icing sugar and syrup in a pan. DO NOT BOIL.
2. Add cocoa and remove from the heat.
3. Use a metal spoon to mix the crispies or cornflakes into the mixture.
4. Place in cake cases.

Can you write the recipe for something else you like to cook? Don't forget to write down what you need and how to cook it.

**Things you need:**

**How to cook:**

# Healthy Eating

Here are some things we all enjoy eating.
Write in their names.

Choose the things that are good for us and cut them out.
Glue them in place in the box and write some words to make a healthy eating poster.

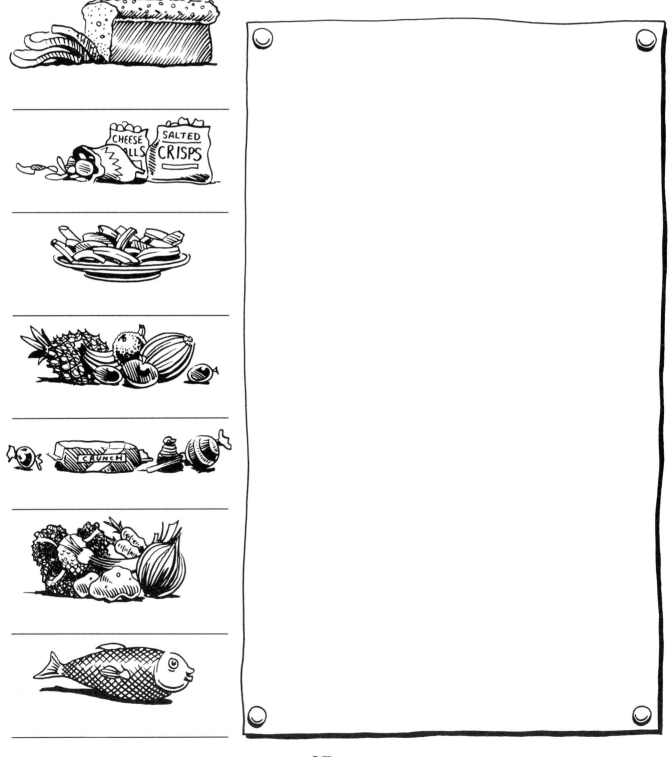

# Food Prayer

What kinds of food do you enjoy eating?

Make up a prayer to say thank you for your food.

**My food prayer**

# School

# Headed Paper

The children and teachers at East Bay School did not like the school headed paper, so they designed their own:

**Before:**

East Bay County Primary School
3 Beach Road
East Bay
SANDMOUTH
Dorset DO12 5AL

Head Teacher: Mrs A Brown BA

**After:**

East Bay
County Primary School
3 Beach Road
East Bay
SANDMOUTH

Head: Angela Brown BA

Design new headed paper for your school.

# Playground Games

Think of something that you play with in the playground. Draw it here and write the name of the game.

_____

Some games can be played without 'things' at all. Can you think of one? Write its name here.

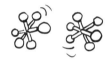

_____

Explain how to play a game that you enjoy.

**A Game I Enjoy**

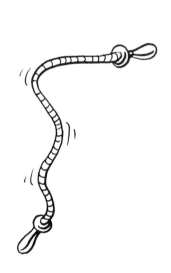

# Make a Book

Think of all the things you like to do in school. Fill in the spaces and draw a picture to go with your writing.

I like to p _ _ _ _

I like to r _ _ _

I like to s _ _ _

I like to p _ _ _

I like to _____

I like to _____

Make more pages for your book.

# Getting Ready for School

Colour the pictures. Put them in order using numbers 1, 2, 3 and 4.

Finish the story.

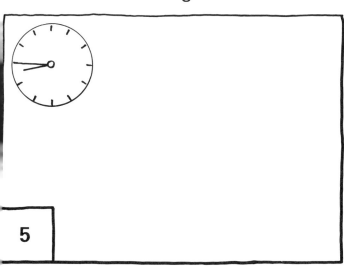

5

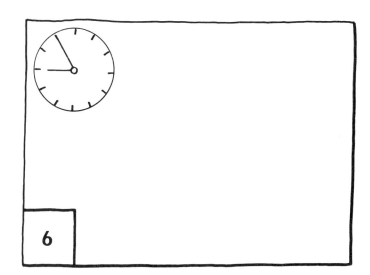

6

# School Rules

Does your school have rules? Can you think of any? Talk about why rules, like this one, are a good idea.

**Don't all shout out!
Put your hand up!**

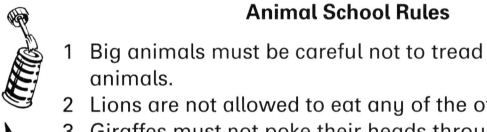

Animal School has to have very special rules. Here are some of them. Can you make up any more?

### Animal School Rules

1 Big animals must be careful not to tread on small animals.
2 Lions are not allowed to eat any of the other pupils.
3 Giraffes must not poke their heads through the ceiling.

# Weather

# Weather Chart

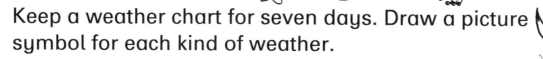

Keep a weather chart for seven days. Draw a picture symbol for each kind of weather.

| Monday | Tuesday | Wednesday | Thursday |
|---|---|---|---|
|  |  |  |  |

| Friday | Saturday | Sunday |
|---|---|---|
|  |  |  |

At the end of the week use your chart to help you write out a weather table.

We had _____ days of _____

We had _____ days of _____

We had _____ days of _____

Write down what the weather was like for most of the week.

_____

Draw pictures to show what kind of clothes you had to wear on each day.

# Weather Invitations

Write an invitation to the snow asking it to fall on Christmas Day.

Find out what day of the week Christmas is this year and put it on your card.

Don't forget to put your address so that the snow knows where to fall.

~ *Invitation* ~

Dear Snow,

## Bear's Clothes

Colour Bear's picture and cut it out very carefully. Design some clothes for Bear to wear. Make clothes for wet days, for sunny days, for cold days.

Don't forget the tabs to fold over his shoulders and around his waist.

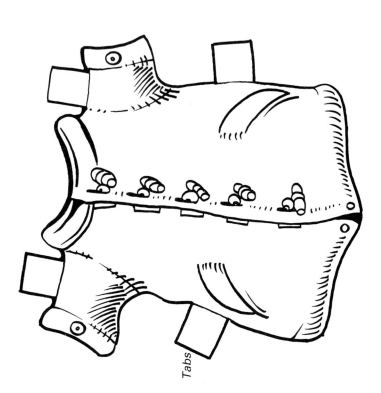

**A coat for a cold day**

# Bear at Granny's House

Bear is going to stay with Granny for a few days' holiday. Write notes for Bear's Granny so that she will know how to dress him for every kind of weather. Draw pictures to help Granny.

**On sunny days Bear wears his**




**On wet days Bear wears his**




**On cold days Bear wears his**




**When Bear goes to the seaside he needs**

# Weather Words

Look at the snow picture. Think of winter days. Think of the cold. Look for words to go with the snow. Write them across the picture. Use some of them to write about a snowy day.

Make a collection of rain words. Write about a very wet day.

Draw pictures of other kinds of weather. Make collections of words to go with the pictures. Write about them.

# Seasons

# Birthday Calendar

Here is part of a birthday calendar for Mrs Winter's class at East Bay School. Can you make a birthday calendar for your class?

**January**
1, 2, 3, 4, 5 Joanne, 6, 7, 8, 9, 10, 11, 12, 13, 14, 15, 16, 17 Mrs Winter, 18, 19, 20, 21, 22, 23, 24, 25 David, 26, 27, 28, 29, 30, 31

**Month:** _____

| 1 | 8 | 15 | 22 | 29 |
|---|---|----|----|----|
| 2 | 9 | 16 | 23 | 30 |
| 3 | 10 | 17 | 24 | 31 |
| 4 | 11 | 18 | 25 | |
| 5 | 12 | 19 | 26 | |
| 6 | 13 | 20 | 27 | |
| 7 | 14 | 21 | 28 | |

# The Apple Tree's Year

## The Apple Tree's Year

Tell the story of the apple tree's year and colour the pictures to go with each season.

Spring • Summer • Autumn • Winter

43

# Harvest Thanksgiving

Make lists of food and flowers we take to school to celebrate Harvest Thanksgiving.

**From the garden**

_____

_____

**From the hedgerows**

_____

_____

**From the shops**

_____

_____

**From the sea**

_____

_____

We took cans of soup to school

Harvest Thanksgiving

We have made a book in the shape of a can of soup. Use your lists to write a sentence about Harvest Thanksgiving on each page. Draw pictures to go with your writing.

# Make a Card

There are special days when we like to send cards to our friends. Can you think of some?

_____

_____

_____

_____

Choose a greeting or make up one of your own. Make a card with a matching picture.

# A Christmas Diary

Think about all the things Father Christmas has to do to get ready for Christmas Day.

Does Mother Christmas help?
Who washes his cloak and cap?
Who feeds the reindeer?
What does Father Christmas do on Christmas Day?

Make up Father Christmas's diary for the days before Christmas.

| **20th December** | **21st December** |
|---|---|
|  |  |
| **22nd December** | **23rd December** |
|  |  |
| **24th December, Christmas Eve** | **25th December, Christmas Day** |
|  |  |

# Colour

## Colour Signals

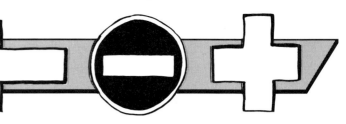

Sometimes colours can tell us what to do.

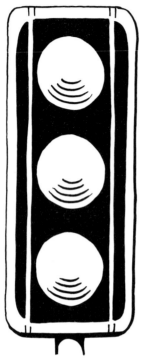

**Red**

**Yellow**

**Green**

**Red says** _____

**Yellow says** _____

**Green says** _____

Can you think of any other messages which colours can give us?

Colour the pictures.

Draw a picture of your street using colours as signals.

# Rainbows

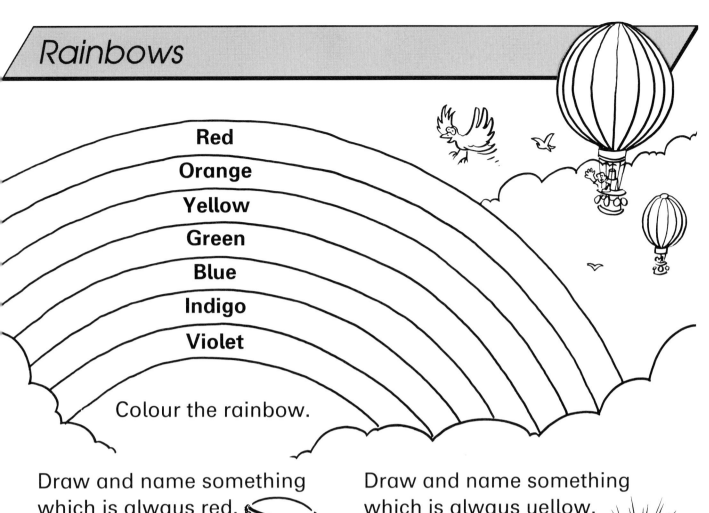

**Red**
**Orange**
**Yellow**
**Green**
**Blue**
**Indigo**
**Violet**

Colour the rainbow.

Draw and name something which is always red.

Draw and name something which is always yellow.

Draw and name something which is always green.
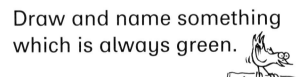

Draw and name something which is always blue.

Can you think of anything that is orange? or indigo? or violet?

| Orange | Indigo | Violet |
|---|---|---|
|  |  |  |

# Invent-a-Colour

Use three different colours, one on top of the other, to make an absolutely new one.

Find an exciting new name for your new colour.

**My new colour is** _____

Write out a recipe for your new colour so that someone else can make it.

# At the End of the Rainbow

There is supposed to be a pot of gold at the end of the rainbow. Sam and Claire see a rainbow. They go on an adventure to find the gold, but it is not as easy as it looks.

Finish Sam and Claire's story.

# Make a Garden

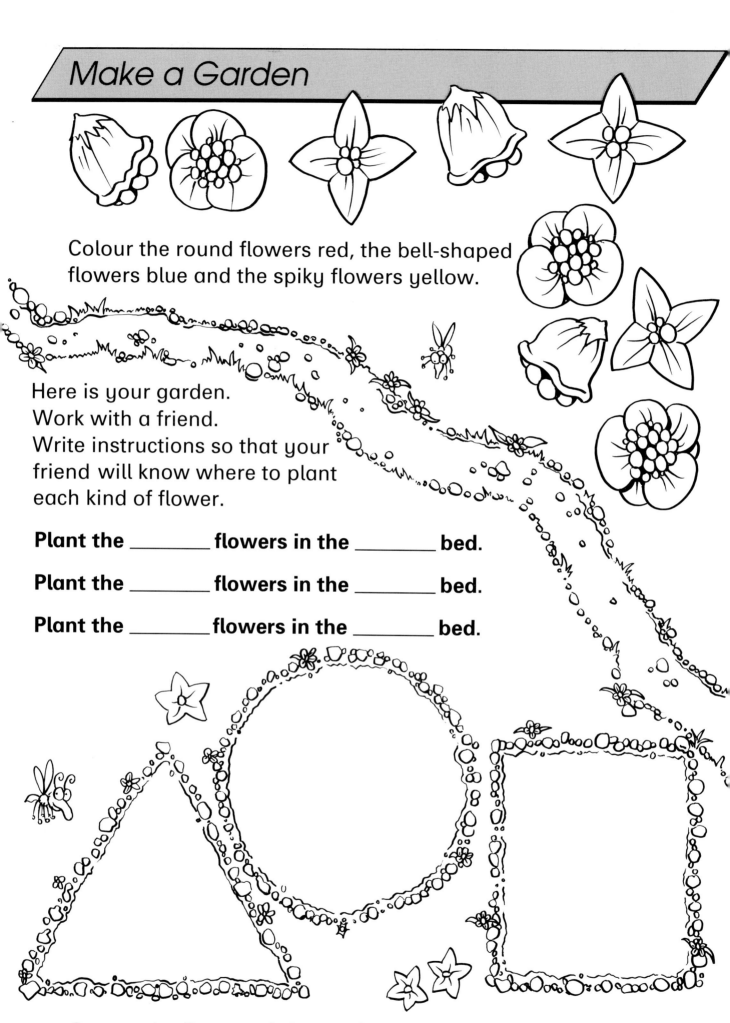

Colour the round flowers red, the bell-shaped flowers blue and the spiky flowers yellow.

Here is your garden.
Work with a friend.
Write instructions so that your friend will know where to plant each kind of flower.

**Plant the** _____ **flowers in the** _____ **bed.**

**Plant the** _____ **flowers in the** _____ **bed.**

**Plant the** _____ **flowers in the** _____ **bed.**

Cut out the flowers. Ask your friend to paste them in the correct bed. See if your friend can follow the instructions.

# Creatures

# Name Me, Draw Me

**I am the biggest animal in the world.**

Draw me

Name me _____

**With my black and white stripes, no one can see me hiding.**

Draw me

Name me _____

Write about me

Name me _____

**With my special pouch, I keep my babies safe.**

Draw me

Name me _____

Write about me

Draw me

Name me _____

Write about me

Name me _____

54

# Into the Ark

Noah has had a busy day loading the ark with animals! Here is part of his diary. Has he chosen good words to tell us how the animals move? Can you help him find better ones?

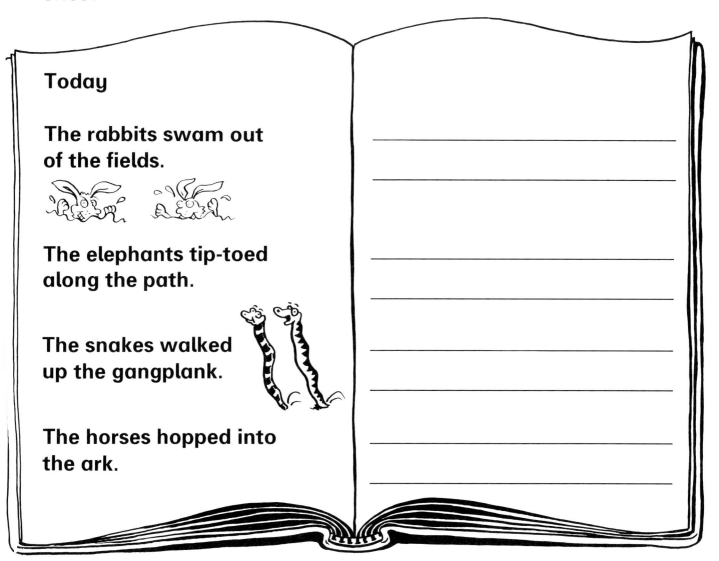

**Today**

**The rabbits swam out of the fields.**

**The elephants tip-toed along the path.**

**The snakes walked up the gangplank.**

**The horses hopped into the ark.**

Make up sentences like these about how other animals move. You could use one of them in a story.

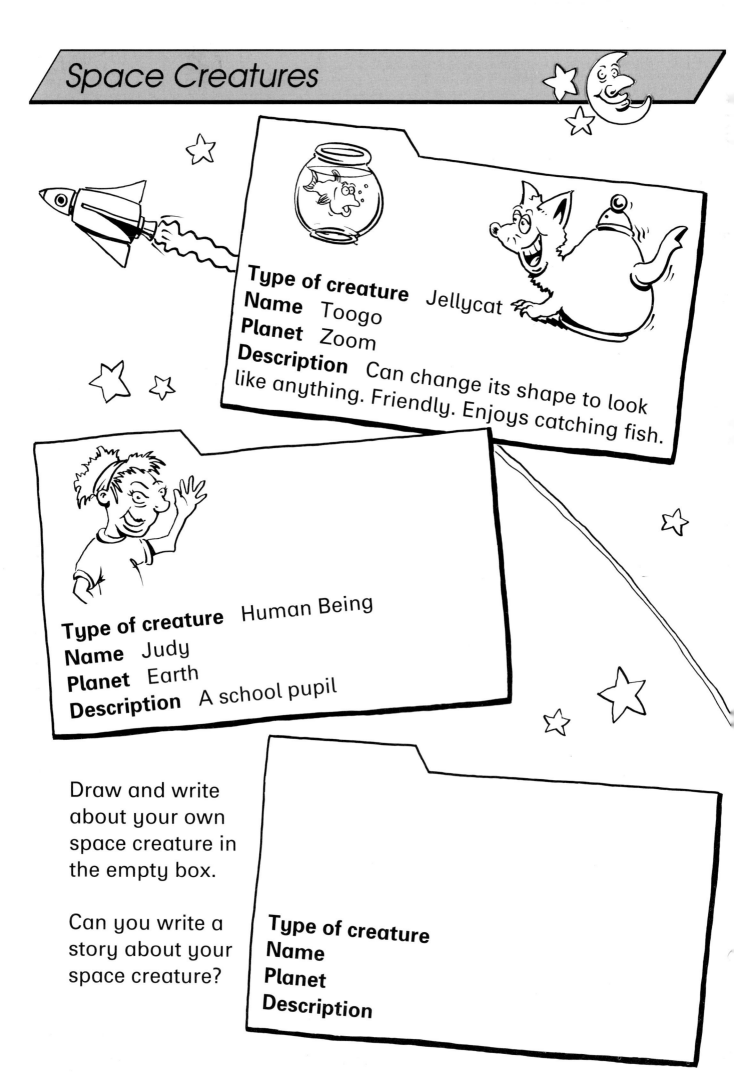

# Recipe for a Monster

Invent your own monster.
Think of all the enormous things that will go to build it.
Write out your ideas like a recipe.

**Things we need:**

head as big as _____

body like a _____

legs as strong as _____

arms made of _____

eyes like _____

and _____

**How to make it:**

_____

_____

_____

_____

Cook for

_____

Decorate with

_____

_____

**Name of monster**

_____

Draw a picture of the monster.

Choose the very smallest creature you can imagine: an ant, a ladybird, a spider, a caterpillar – or something else.

Find out all about its home, its friends, what it likes to eat. Make notes.

Tell the very small creature's story in its own very small book. Use your notes.

Cut

**A Very Small Creature's Story**

Cut